This Maid Of Honor Organizer Belongs To:

_____

DEDICATION

This book is dedicated to all the spectacular Maid of Honor's out there who want to be the best Maid of Honor they can be.

Your are my inspiration for producing books
and I'm honored to be a part of keeping all your Maid of Honor notes & records organized.

This journal notebook will help you record your details and experiences as an awesome Maid of Honor.

Thoughtfully put together with these sections to record Important Dates At A Glance, Master To Do List, Monthly Planner, Weekly Planner, Bridal Party Contact List, Vendor Contact List, Bridal Shower Budget, Bridal Shower Planner, Bachelorette Party Budget, Bachelorette Party Planner, Wedding Day Emergency Kit and Notes, Ideas & Memories.

I hope you enjoy being the Maid of Honor!

HOW TO USE THIS BOOK:

The purpose of this book is to keep all of your Maid of Honor notes, ideas and planning all in one place. It will help keep you organized.

This Maid of Honor Planner will allow you to accurately document and plan all the things you want to remember about your experience and privilege as Maid of Honor. It's a great way to chart your course as Maid of Honor.

Here are examples of the prompts for you to fill in and write about your experience of planning in this book:

1. Important Dates At A Glance - Wedding date, save the date mailing by, dress shopping, bridal shower, invitations mailed by, bachelorette party, wedding day hair/nails.
2. Master To-Do List - Tick box checklist to write things to remember & do.
3. Monthly Planner - Undated calendar (6 months) to look at the month at a glance.
4. Weekly Planner - Will help plan your week with to do list, any appointments & notes.
5. Bridal Party Contact List - Name, cell, email, role.
6. Vendor Contact Lists - Wedding cake, ceremony & reception venue, entertainment, officiant, florist, caterer, limo/transportation, em cee, photographer, videographer, alterations.
7. Bridal Shower Budget - Tracker that you can track your spending for: invitations, venue, food & drink, decorations, favor & games, entertainment.
8. Bridal Shower Planner - Party details, games & activities, food & drink, decorations, guest list, shopping list.
9. Bachelorette Party Budget - Tracker that you can track your spending for: invitations, venue, food & drink, decorations, favor & games, entertainment.
10. Bachelorette Party Planner - Party details, games & activities, food & drink, decorations, guest list, shopping list.
11. Wedding Day Emergency Kit - Checklist for things to pack to ensure you're prepared for any emergency.
12. Notes/ Ideas/ Memories - Blank lined pages to use for anything you wish to write or just want to remember.

Important Dates At A Glance

Wedding Date _____

Save The Date Mailing By _____

Coordinate Gift Registry _____

Dress Shopping _____

Meeting With Caterer _____

Invitations Mailed By _____

Bridal Shower _____

Final Dress Alterations _____

Finalize Guest List _____

Bachelorette Party _____

Wedding Day Hair/Nails _____

Master To-Do List

☐ _____
☐ _____
☐ _____
☐ _____
☐ _____
☐ _____
☐ _____
☐ _____
☐ _____
☐ _____
☐ _____
☐ _____
☐ _____
☐ _____
☐ _____
☐ _____
☐ _____

☐ _____
☐ _____
☐ _____
☐ _____
☐ _____
☐ _____
☐ _____
☐ _____
☐ _____
☐ _____
☐ _____
☐ _____
☐ _____
☐ _____
☐ _____
☐ _____
☐ _____

Monthly Planner

Month Of:_____

SUN	MON	TUES	WED	THURS	FRI	SAT

Monthly Planner

Month Of:_____

SUN	MON	TUES	WED	THURS	FRI	SAT

Monthly Planner

Month Of:_____

SUN	MON	TUES	WED	THURS	FRI	SAT

Monthly *Planner*

Month Of:_____

SUN	MON	TUES	WED	THURS	FRI	SAT

Monthly Planner

Month Of:_____

SUN	MON	TUES	WED	THURS	FRI	SAT

Monthly Planner

Month Of:_____

SUN	MON	TUES	WED	THURS	FRI	SAT

Weekly Planner

Sunday

Monday

Tuesday

Wednesday

Thursday

Friday

Saturday

Week Of:_____

To Do List:

- [ ]
- [ ]
- [ ]
- [ ]
- [ ]

APPOINTMENTS

Date	Time	Vendor	Contact Info

Notes

Weekly Planner

Sunday	Week Of:_____

Sunday

Monday

Tuesday

Wednesday

Thursday

Friday

Saturday

To Do List:

☐ _____

☐ _____

☐ _____

☐ _____

☐ _____

APPOINTMENTS

Date	Time	Vendor	Contact Info

Notes

Weekly Planner

Sunday

Monday

Tuesday

Wednesday

Thursday

Friday

Saturday

Week Of:_____

To Do List:

- ☐
- ☐
- ☐
- ☐
- ☐

APPOINTMENTS

Date	Time	Vendor	Contact Info

Notes

Weekly Planner

Sunday	Week Of:_____

Sunday

Monday

Tuesday

Wednesday

Thursday

Friday

Saturday

To Do List:

- [ ]
- [ ]
- [ ]
- [ ]
- [ ]

APPOINTMENTS

Date	Time	Vendor	Contact Info

Notes

Weekly Planner

Sunday

Monday

Tuesday

Wednesday

Thursday

Friday

Saturday

Week Of:_____

To Do List:

- ☐
- ☐
- ☐
- ☐
- ☐

APPOINTMENTS

Date	Time	Vendor	Contact Info

Notes

Weekly *Planner*

| Sunday | Week Of:_____ |

Sunday

Monday

Tuesday

Wednesday

Thursday

Friday

Saturday

To Do List:

- ☐ _____
- ☐ _____
- ☐ _____
- ☐ _____
- ☐ _____

APPOINTMENTS

Date	Time	Vendor	Contact Info

Notes

Weekly Planner

Sunday

Monday

Tuesday

Wednesday

Thursday

Friday

Saturday

Week Of:_____

To Do List:

- [ ]
- [ ]
- [ ]
- [ ]
- [ ]

APPOINTMENTS

Date	Time	Vendor	Contact Info

Notes

Weekly Planner

Sunday

| Monday |

| Tuesday |

| Wednesday |

| Thursday |

| Friday |

| Saturday |

Week Of:_____

To Do List:

☐ _____
☐ _____
☐ _____
☐ _____
☐ _____

APPOINTMENTS

Date	Time	Vendor	Contact Info

Notes

Weekly Planner

Sunday

Monday

Tuesday

Wednesday

Thursday

Friday

Saturday

Week Of:_____

To Do List:

- [ ]
- [ ]
- [ ]
- [ ]
- [ ]

APPOINTMENTS

Date	Time	Vendor	Contact Info

Notes

Weekly *Planner*

Sunday	**Week Of:**_____

Sunday	
Monday	
Tuesday	
Wednesday	
Thursday	
Friday	
Saturday	

To Do List:

☐ _____

☐ _____

☐ _____

☐ _____

☐ _____

APPOINTMENTS

Date	Time	Vendor	Contact Info

Notes

Weekly Planner

Sunday	Week Of:_____

To Do List:

- ☐ _____
- ☐ _____
- ☐ _____
- ☐ _____
- ☐ _____

Monday

Tuesday

APPOINTMENTS

Date	Time	Vendor	Contact Info

Wednesday

Thursday

Notes

Friday

Saturday

Weekly Planner

Sunday	Week Of:_____

Sunday

Monday

Tuesday

Wednesday

Thursday

Friday

Saturday

To Do List:

☐ _____
☐ _____
☐ _____
☐ _____
☐ _____

APPOINTMENTS

Date	Time	Vendor	Contact Info

Notes

Weekly Planner

Sunday
Monday
Tuesday
Wednesday
Thursday
Friday
Saturday

Week Of:_____

To Do List:

- [ ]
- [ ]
- [ ]
- [ ]
- [ ]

APPOINTMENTS

Date	Time	Vendor	Contact Info

Notes

Weekly Planner

| Sunday | Week Of:_____ |

Sunday

Monday

Tuesday

Wednesday

Thursday

Friday

Saturday

To Do List:

- ☐
- ☐
- ☐
- ☐
- ☐

APPOINTMENTS

Date	Time	Vendor	Contact Info

Notes

Weekly Planner

Sunday	Week Of:_____

Sunday

Monday

Tuesday

Wednesday

Thursday

Friday

Saturday

To Do List:

- ☐
- ☐
- ☐
- ☐
- ☐

APPOINTMENTS

Date	Time	Vendor	Contact Info

Notes

Weekly Planner

Sunday	Week Of: _____

Sunday

Monday

Tuesday

Wednesday

Thursday

Friday

Saturday

To Do List:

☐ _____
☐ _____
☐ _____
☐ _____
☐ _____

APPOINTMENTS

Date	Time	Vendor	Contact Info

Notes

Weekly Planner

Sunday

Monday

Tuesday

Wednesday

Thursday

Friday

Saturday

Week Of:_____

To Do List:

☐
☐
☐
☐
☐

APPOINTMENTS

Date	Time	Vendor	Contact Info

Notes

Weekly Planner

Sunday

Monday

Tuesday

Wednesday

Thursday

Friday

Saturday

Week Of:_____

To Do List:

- [ ] _____
- [ ] _____
- [ ] _____
- [ ] _____
- [ ] _____

APPOINTMENTS

Date	Time	Vendor	Contact Info

Notes

Weekly Planner

Sunday

Monday

Tuesday

Wednesday

Thursday

Friday

Saturday

Week Of:_____

To Do List:

- [ ]
- [ ]
- [ ]
- [ ]
- [ ]

APPOINTMENTS

Date	Time	Vendor	Contact Info

Notes

Weekly Planner

Sunday	Week Of:_____

Sunday

Monday

Tuesday

Wednesday

Thursday

Friday

Saturday

To Do List:

☐

☐

☐

☐

☐

APPOINTMENTS

Date	Time	Vendor	Contact Info

Notes

Weekly $Planner$

Sunday

Monday

Tuesday

Wednesday

Thursday

Friday

Saturday

Week Of:_____

To Do List:

- ☐
- ☐
- ☐
- ☐
- ☐

APPOINTMENTS

Date	Time	Vendor	Contact Info

Notes

Weekly *Planner*

| Sunday | Week Of:_____ |

To Do List:

☐ _____

☐ _____

☐ _____

☐ _____

☐ _____

Sunday

Monday

Tuesday

Wednesday

Thursday

Friday

Saturday

APPOINTMENTS

Date	Time	Vendor	Contact Info

Notes

Weekly Planner

Sunday

Monday

Tuesday

Wednesday

Thursday

Friday

Saturday

Week Of:_____

To Do List:

- ☐
- ☐
- ☐
- ☐
- ☐

APPOINTMENTS

Date	Time	Vendor	Contact Info

Notes

Weekly Planner

Sunday
Monday
Tuesday
Wednesday
Thursday
Friday
Saturday

Week Of:_____

To Do List:

- ☐
- ☐
- ☐
- ☐
- ☐

APPOINTMENTS

Date	Time	Vendor	Contact Info

Notes

Weekly Planner

| Sunday | Week Of: _____ |

To Do List:

- ☐ _____
- ☐ _____
- ☐ _____
- ☐ _____
- ☐ _____

Monday

Tuesday

APPOINTMENTS

Date	Time	Vendor	Contact Info

Wednesday

Thursday

Notes

Friday

Saturday

Weekly *Planner*

Sunday

Monday

Tuesday

Wednesday

Thursday

Friday

Saturday

Week Of:_____

To Do List:

- [ ]
- [ ]
- [ ]
- [ ]
- [ ]

APPOINTMENTS

Date	Time	Vendor	Contact Info

Notes

Weekly Planner

Sunday

Monday

Tuesday

Wednesday

Thursday

Friday

Saturday

Week Of:_____

To Do List:

- [ ]
- [ ]
- [ ]
- [ ]
- [ ]

APPOINTMENTS

Date	Time	Vendor	Contact Info

Notes

Weekly Planner

Sunday	Week Of:_____

To Do List:

- [ ] _____
- [ ] _____
- [ ] _____
- [ ] _____
- [ ] _____

Monday

Tuesday

APPOINTMENTS

Date	Time	Vendor	Contact Info

Wednesday

Thursday

Notes

Friday

Saturday

Weekly Planner

Sunday

Monday

Tuesday

Wednesday

Thursday

Friday

Saturday

Week Of:_____

To Do List:

- ☐
- ☐
- ☐
- ☐
- ☐

APPOINTMENTS

Date	Time	Vendor	Contact Info

Notes

Weekly Planner

Sunday	Week Of: _____

Sunday

Monday

Tuesday

Wednesday

Thursday

Friday

Saturday

To Do List:

☐ _____
☐ _____
☐ _____
☐ _____
☐ _____

APPOINTMENTS

Date	Time	Vendor	Contact Info

Notes

Bridal Party Contact List

Name:

Cell:

Email:

Role:

Name:

Cell:

Email:

Role:

Name:

Cell:

Email:

Role:

Name:

Cell:

Email:

Role:

Name:

Cell:

Email:

Role:

Name:

Cell:

Email:

Role:

Name:

Cell:

Email:

Role:

Name:

Cell:

Email:

Role:

Name:

Cell:

Email:

Role:

Name:

Cell:

Email:

Role:

Bridal Party Contact List

Name:

Cell:

Email:

Role:

Name:

Cell:

Email:

Role:

Name:

Cell:

Email:

Role:

Name:

Cell:

Email:

Role:

Name:

Cell:

Email:

Role:

Name:

Cell:

Email:

Role:

Name:

Cell:

Email:

Role:

Name:

Cell:

Email:

Role:

Name:

Cell:

Email:

Role:

Name:

Cell:

Email:

Role:

Vendor Contact List

WEDDING CAKE

Vendor:

Contact:

Email:

Phone:

Notes:

CEREMONY VENUE

Vendor:

Contact:

Email:

Phone:

Notes:

RECEPTION ENTERTAINMENT

Vendor:

Contact:

Email:

Phone:

Notes:

RECEPTION VENUE

Vendor:

Contact:

Email:

Phone:

Notes:

Vendor Contact List

BACHELORETTE PARTY VENUE

Vendor:

Contact:

Email:

Phone:

Notes:

WEDDING HAIR

Vendor:

Contact:

Email:

Phone:

Notes:

WEDDING NAILS

Vendor:

Contact:

Email:

Phone:

Notes:

CEREMONY OFFICIANT

Vendor:

Contact:

Email:

Phone:

Notes:

Vendor Contact List

FLORIST

Vendor:

Contact:

Email:

Phone:

Notes:

CATERER

Vendor:

Contact:

Email:

Phone:

Notes:

EM CEE

Vendor:

Contact:

Email:

Phone:

Notes:

LIMO/TRANSPORTATION

Vendor:

Contact:

Email:

Phone:

Notes:

Vendor Contact List

WEDDING COORDINATOR

Vendor:

Contact:

Email:

Phone:

Notes:

PHOTOGRAPHER

Vendor:

Contact:

Email:

Phone:

Notes:

VIDEOGRAPHER

Vendor:

Contact:

Email:

Phone:

Notes:

ALTERATIONS

Vendor:

Contact:

Email:

Phone:

Notes:

Vendor Contact List

Vendor:

Contact:

Email:

Phone:

Notes:

_____

_____

_____

_____

Vendor:

Contact:

Email:

Phone:

Notes:

_____

_____

_____

_____

Vendor:

Contact:

Email:

Phone:

Notes:

_____

_____

_____

_____

Vendor:

Contact:

Email:

Phone:

Notes:

_____

_____

_____

_____

Vendor Contact List

Vendor: _____

Contact: _____

Email: _____

Phone: _____

Notes: _____

_____

_____

_____

Vendor: _____

Contact: _____

Email: _____

Phone: _____

Notes: _____

_____

_____

_____

Vendor: _____

Contact: _____

Email: _____

Phone: _____

Notes: _____

_____

_____

_____

Vendor: _____

Contact: _____

Email: _____

Phone: _____

Notes: _____

_____

_____

_____

Bridal Shower Budget

Total Budget _____

CATEGORY	BUDGET	ACTUAL COST	DEPOSIT PAID	BALANCE	DUE
INVITATIONS					
Save The Date					
Invitations					
Envelopes					
Thank You Cards					
Postage					
VENUE					
Rental Fee					
Misc.					
FOOD & DRINK					
Catering					
Beverages					
Alcoholic					
Non-alcoholic					
Cake					
Plates/Bowls					
Utensils					
Napkins					

Bridal Shower Budget

CATEGORY	BUDGET	ACTUAL COST	DEPOSIT PAID	BALANCE	DUE
DECORATIONS					
Table Decorations					
Venue Decorations					
Signs, Banners, Wall Decor					
Misc. Decorations					
FAVORS & GAMES					
Games					
Prizes					
Favors					
ENTERTAINMENT					
OTHER					

Bridal Shower Planner

PARTY DETAILS
DATE
TIME
VENUE
THEME
NOTES

GAMES/ACTIVITIES

Food/Drink

Decorations

GUEST LIST

NAME	CONTACT INFO	RSVP

GUEST LIST		
NAME	CONTACT INFO	RSVP

Shopping List

- [ ] _____
- [ ] _____
- [ ] _____
- [ ] _____
- [ ] _____
- [ ] _____
- [ ] _____
- [ ] _____
- [ ] _____
- [ ] _____
- [ ] _____
- [ ] _____
- [ ] _____
- [ ] _____
- [ ] _____
- [ ] _____

- [ ] _____
- [ ] _____
- [ ] _____
- [ ] _____
- [ ] _____
- [ ] _____
- [ ] _____
- [ ] _____
- [ ] _____
- [ ] _____
- [ ] _____
- [ ] _____
- [ ] _____
- [ ] _____
- [ ] _____
- [ ] _____

Bachelorette Party Budget

Total Budget _____

CATEGORY	BUDGET	ACTUAL COST	DEPOSIT PAID	BALANCE	DUE
INVITATIONS					
Save The Date					
Invitations					
Envelopes					
Thank You Cards					
Postage					
VENUE					
Rental Fee					
Misc.					
FOOD & DRINK					
Catering					
Beverages					
Alcoholic					
Non-alcoholic					
Cake					
Plates/Bowls					
Utensils					
Napkins					

Bachelorette Party Budget

CATEGORY	BUDGET	ACTUAL COST	DEPOSIT PAID	BALANCE	DUE
DECORATIONS					
Table Decorations					
Venue Decorations					
Signs, Banners, Wall Decor					
Misc. Decorations					
FAVORS & GAMES					
Games					
Prizes					
Favors					
ENTERTAINMENT					
OTHER					

Bachelorette Party Planner

PARTY DETAILS	
DATE	
TIME	
VENUE	
THEME	
NOTES	

GAMES/ACTIVITIES

Food/Drink

Decorations

GUEST LIST		
NAME	CONTACT INFO	RSVP

GUEST LIST		
NAME	CONTACT INFO	RSVP

Shopping List

☐ _____

☐ _____

☐ _____

☐ _____

☐ _____

☐ _____

☐ _____

☐ _____

☐ _____

☐ _____

☐ _____

☐ _____

☐ _____

☐ _____

☐ _____

☐ _____

☐ _____

☐ _____

☐ _____

☐ _____

☐ _____

☐ _____

☐ _____

☐ _____

☐ _____

☐ _____

☐ _____

☐ _____

☐ _____

☐ _____

Wedding Day Emergency Kit

Apparel Repair Kit

- [ ] Small Scissors
- [ ] Safety Pins
- [ ] Hem Tape
- [ ] Clear Nail Polish
- [ ] Tide-To-Go
- [ ] Lint Roller
- [ ] Sewing Kit

Hair

- [ ] Comb/Brush
- [ ] Bobby Pins
- [ ] Hair Ties
- [ ] Hairspray
- [ ] Dry Shampoo
- [ ] Hair Straightener/Curling Iron

Toiletries

- [ ] Q-Tips
- [ ] Tweezers
- [ ] Nail File
- [ ] Touch-up Nail Polish
- [ ] Deodorant
- [ ] Perfume
- [ ] Tissues
- [ ] Tampons/Pads
- [ ] Toothbrush/Paste/Floss
- [ ] Lotion

Meds/First Aid

- [ ] Antacid
- [ ] Band-Aids
- [ ] Tylenol/Motrin
- [ ] Contact Solution
- [ ] Allergy Medicine
- [ ] Bug Spray

Notes/Ideas/Memories

Notes/Ideas/Memories

Notes/Ideas/Memories

Notes/Ideas/Memories

Notes/Ideas/Memories

Notes/Ideas/Memories

Notes/Ideas/Memories

Notes/Ideas/Memories

Notes/Ideas/Memories

Notes/Ideas/Memories

Notes/Ideas/Memories

Notes/Ideas/Memories

Notes/Ideas/Memories

Notes/Ideas/Memories

Notes/Ideas/Memories

Notes/Ideas/Memories

Notes/Ideas/Memories

Notes/Ideas/Memories

Notes/Ideas/Memories

Notes/Ideas/Memories

Notes/Ideas/Memories

Notes/Ideas/Memories

Notes/Ideas/Memories

Notes/Ideas/Memories

Notes/Ideas/Memories

Notes/Ideas/Memories

Notes/Ideas/Memories

Notes/Ideas/Memories

Notes/Ideas/Memories

Notes/Ideas/Memories

Notes/Ideas/Memories

Notes/Ideas/Memories

Notes/Ideas/Memories

Notes/Ideas/Memories

Notes/Ideas/Memories

Notes/Ideas/Memories

Notes/Ideas/Memories

Notes/Ideas/Memories

Notes/Ideas/Memories

Notes/Ideas/Memories

Notes/Ideas/Memories

Notes/Ideas/Memories

Notes/Ideas/Memories

Notes/Ideas/Memories

Notes/Ideas/Memories

Notes/Ideas/Memories

Notes/Ideas/Memories

Notes/Ideas/Memories